# Shine Light on Mental Fights

Charley Johnson

———∿∘०ℰⴲ◑◐Ⴒℰ०∘∿———

I would like to acknowledge those who helped me along the way while I was writing this book. I could not have done this without the support of my mother and all those around me. Hearing my friends cheer me along in my writing journey really pushed me further and made this dream become a reality. I would also like to thank Alana. She is an amazing role model, and I am so thankful for her help with the sketches inside my book. She really helped me get my ideas onto paper, when I couldn't on my own. And they look better than I could have ever imagined. I am also so grateful for my editors and designers, everyone who has helped make the writing and publishing process easier than I ever thought it could be. Finally I owe a big thank you to Michelle Prince. She was such an inspiration, helping with the formation of my book idea, getting my ideas onto paper, and helping me start my writing journey. She has helped me realize my love for writing and how important it is to share my message, even if it only touches one person. I am unbelievably thankful for all of the support I had in writing this book. Thank you.

Sketches by: Alaina Lohr
Photographer: Bobby Barron

———∿∘०ℰⴲ◑◐Ⴒℰ०∘∿———

# Contents

# Body Shame

Words like knives
    Breaking you down,
For believing there is a "perfect" type of body,
You have been ripped of your crown.

You compare yourself to models
And feel you are worth less,
But no one can look the same.
So how can people go and shame?

Too fat, too skinny,
Too tall, too short,
Trying your hardest to receive fame,
But putting yourself through so much pain.

Eat less. You don't need the weight.
Eat more. You can see your bones.
You once used to smile when you saw your reflection.
Now all you can do is point out your imperfections.

Day after day,
You skip all your meals.
To have a better body,
For others' appeal.

No matter what you do, you can do more
To look like a Barbie from the store.
You need to look "fake" for people to like you,
For if you have no friends and fans, what will you do?

You can't take the pressure anymore
To be perfect for others' pleasure.
The words, they weigh you down.
The pressure suffocates you, as you try and look profound.

This world we live in can't see beauty,
For everyone has it in their own way.
But without the acceptance of others,
Some don't make it to see the next day.

We focus too much on how we can be the best
But neglect others who need rest,
Rest from all the hurtful words
They face every day without being heard.

Some words can bring you down,
But you should focus on the ones that lift you off the ground,
The ones that lift you up and make you smile
And help you learn to go the extra mile.

Making someone's day better with very few words
Could save someone's life and make them feel heard.

We are all different in our own way,
And the kindness of one person could make someone's whole day.

*Charley Johnson*

# Eating Disorders

The number on the scale,
  Glares back at you.
Judging your weight,
You hate the view.

You've tried working out.
It still seemed to rise.
What am I doing wrong?
How can this be right?

Nothing seemed to work,
So maybe just one meal.
It really won't hurt.
So what's the big deal?

You start skipping breakfast,
From that day on.
Starting to see results,
You grow very fond.

Why didn't I think of this before?
It really helps,
But it doesn't help enough,
You go back to how you felt.

Maybe just one more,
And it'll all be good.
Then I'll look thin,
The way I should.

Down to one meal,
Just one meal a day.
It's hard at first,
But that feeling goes away.

You start to grow weak.
But why should you care?
You are finally looking pretty.
People stop to stare.

You feed off this attention.
It fuels your every move.
You have little energy,
From your lack of real food.

The results start to slow.
Then they come to a halt.
How can this be?
Am I the one at fault?

The figure in the mirror still upsets you.
This is not what I want. What can I do?

Maybe just one meal,
One meal every other day.
I can't think of anything else.
There is no other way.

Weaker and weaker, you start to grow.
You begin to feel helpless, like a stranded foe.

You are never pleased with the figure in the mirror.
Your insecurities just start to become much clearer.

*Charley Johnson*

The sight of food becomes a fright.
So many calories and fat,
Just for one bite.

The trouble starts when you can't remember the last time you ate.
Could this lead to your fate?

Is this all really worth the few extra likes?
The suffering and pain,
The agony and shame.

No longer able to eat full meals,
All because of wanting a better body for others' appeal.

This distorted image you believe is perfection
Leaves you with unrealistic perceptions.

All because of a want to fit in,
You have to live with the effects.
No longer able to eat right,
Never given a rest.

Maybe just one meal
To create a better body for others' appeal.
This new body isn't for you.
It's for the acceptance of others and what they want to view.

The number on the scale will never go away.
Work on you for you, and not because of what others say.

# *Depression*

K eep it inside
   Bury it down
Maintain your pride
Don't make a sound

Fake it till you make it
That's what you're taught right?
Killing you slowly
Unable to put up a fight

Wear a smile
Push your feelings aside
For society couldn't care less
If you feel like you're dying inside

Your thoughts eat you alive
Picking you apart piece by piece
Tricking your mind
Into believing you are cheap

Breaking down when you are all alone
Afraid to express your feelings
Even in your own home

Feeling you don't do enough
But not willing to do more
Missing out from everyday society
Having no energy to store

*Charley Johnson*

This empty feeling just becomes stronger
You ignore its calling
But it tries harder

Screaming out for help
It wants to be heard
But you keep it deep down
Never speaking a word

I'm ok, I'm fine
Lies you tell those who care
You don't wanna seem pathetic
But you just wanna share

Listening to others when they need a hand
But never opening up
Never letting them in

Thinking of if you should speak the truth
Causes you to become hesitant
But you know you will get hurt
So why even question it?

Keep it inside
Bury it deep
Ignore what's wrong
Don't make a peep

Don't show weakness
You'll just get hurt
Be like a soldier
Stay alert

Hurtful words will find a way in
They will make your bones grow very thin
Making you weak without even knowing
None of your suffering ever showing

You don't realize it till you lose all emotion
Feeling empty and unaffected
Like a very still ocean

Once it enters it never goes away
You just learn to ignore it more with each day

Keep it inside
Bury it down
Live with the pain
Don't make a sound

*Charley Johnson*

# Self-Harm

S ilver.
Back and forth glides the blade
One cut for your every mistake
Cutting as much as you can take

Thick red blood
Covers your towels
Running down your body
No one around

The pain is just a thought
An unimportant belief
That you're really not ok
You tremble to your feet

Down your legs it runs
The beads of blood a relief
That you got what you deserved
At least that's what you think

Shaky hands as you grip the blade
Remembering those who didn't stay

This weapon you bare
Makes you weak and vulnerable
It should not be used for harming
The person behind the handle

Trembling knees as you rise to your feet
The cold rag skimming
Over cuts that run deep

Just one cut
One for your every mistake
Sleeves cover the scars
You are such a fake

Wearing a smile
You pretend to be ok
But the pain just grows deeper
With each passing day

The scars are a constant reminder of all of your faults
Worsening the perception you have of yourself
Messing with your thoughts

This need to feel pain just gets worse
Needing the torture,
Needing the hurt

With each extra cut
You can tolerate more
Adding to the amount of cuts
You have a need for

Hiding your body
So no one can see
The pain and suffering
That lies just beneath

*Charley Johnson*

Beneath the long sleeves
And the grey sweatpants
You don't feel sorry
You don't even glance

Just one cut
For everything you've done wrong
You are a mistake
You don't belong

Back into hiding
The silver blade goes
Wiping tears from your face
So nobody knows

# Drugs

S haky legs
  Wobbly feet
Walk the line
In the street

It didn't seem like much
Just a few cups
It helped you forget about everything
For just a few bucks

Drink after drink
Shot after shot
Doesn't matter you're underaged
You didn't get caught

The alcoholic beverages
Kept the pain away
It helped you forget about
What eats at you every day

It's not an addiction
At least that's what you think
You start doing it more often
Thinking it will only be "one drink"

You crave the feeling
The burn as it goes down
After all it does no harm
It's just a "night out on the town"

*Charley Johnson*

Because of all the drinks
And all of the shots
You no longer think about them
Not even a thought

All the bad in your life
It fades as you drink more
You finally feel free
A feeling you adore

The more you drink
The less it helps
It's not strong enough
You're back to your normal self

You need something more
Something stronger
To rid the pain
You can't take it any longer

Indulging in more
You move from drug to drug
Nothing fills the hole in your heart
You just need a hug

A hug and for someone to tell you it will all be ok
Would help with what you suffer from every day

Nothing seems to help
It just makes you feel more empty
Broke and alone
On the street with no home

The world becomes too much
You can no longer bear the pain
There's only one option left
Nothing will ever change

Two pills
The serving size for one
You dump the rest of the bottle into your hand

A cup of water
And one swallow
Now it's over.

*Charley Johnson*

# Anxiety

Lazy today.
Failure tomorrow.
Time moves so fast,
You feel as if you don't make enough of an impact.

Day after day,
It's the same routine.
You aren't really "living,"
Just staying alive.

You don't make new friends,
But who really knows you anyways?
You're just another person,
Just another being.

Stress about the past.
Worry about the future.
You can't control either,
Yet you chose to spend all your time trying.

Trying to control the uncontrollable,
Trying to fix what's already passed,
You try and try,
But nothing is enough.

Enough to slow your thoughts,
To silence your brain,
Nothing can suffocate the voice.
It never gets quiet.

The voice that tells you, you don't do enough
Or reminds you of your worst moments,
Even though surely no one remembers.
But the voice holds it over you.

It knows your weak spots,
What makes you vulnerable,
Like a blade in your chest
And you are holding the handle.

The voice never quiets.
It always has something to say,
Something to make you worry.
It will always have the upper hand.

It nags at your insecurities
And pushes you over the edge.
You can't take its constant pushing.
It's like it's constantly trying to push you off a ledge.

Only you can stop the pushing,
For it's your own actions.
No one knows you better.
You know what hurts most.

You are the nagging voice,
And you think it's just "fear."
But you are just making yourself frightful,
Afraid of the uncontrollable.

*Charley Johnson*

You think everyone's looking,
So you worry what you look like,
Stressing about judgment.

But everyone is so consumed with the worry of judgment.
No one has time to judge.

You are the voice.
You control what it says.
Remember that
Before it gets to your head.

# Fake Friends

You surround yourself with people,
People who are supposed to make you the "better version of yourself."
But what if they are just there to fill the loneliness?
They don't actually care about you,
But you keep them there so you don't have to be alone.

They talk behind your back,
But you already knew that.
They have a group chat with everyone in it besides you.
But that's ok, because without them you have no one.

I mean yes, you are always the one walking behind them when there's only room for two on the sidewalk.
And yes, you are the one to sleep on the floor at the sleepover because the bed is "made for two."
But that's ok because at least you're there.

You could never talk to them about your crush,
Because the whole school would know by noon.
But at least they know your favorite color.

They are never the friends to ask "Are you ok?"
But they will go to the mall with you.
They may have had other plans on your birthday,
But that's ok because at least you got invited to theirs.

You'll never be their first choice,
But that's ok because at least you're an option.
They will always be the duo,
And you'll always be the third wheel

*Charley Johnson*

But that's ok.
It has to be ok.
Yeah.
Because you don't know what it's like to have a "best friend."

You don't know what it's like for someone to ask how your day
was,
Nor do you know what it's like to be on FaceTime all night
Or what it's like to talk about boys and have the most amazing
conversations.

You don't know what that's like because you are just an "extra"
in their world,
The one they just keep around.

You don't know what it's like to feel wanted,
And it's not ok.
But you have to accept it
For that's the way it'll always be.

Just my fake friends and me.

# Social Media

L ikes and follows
A priority for most
A daily hashtag
And a bunch of new posts

It started off fun
You could see everyone's daily lives
Commenting on how cute their outfit was
Made you feel good inside

Watching reels
And sharing memes
Was very fun
Or so it seemed

You grow the need to check your socials
Every hour or two
To make sure you didn't miss anything
But this need only grew

It hurt when you don't get as many likes
Or when somebody unfollowed
You blamed yourself
And it was a hard pill to swallow

Thinking all these people hated you
Really hurt
Breaking your self-confidence
You felt like dirt

*Charley Johnson*

You see posts of models
And all the comments on how they are perfection
It changes the way you see yourself
Your whole perception

Your perception of what beauty is
You never look at yourself the same
For you're not nearly as pretty
You start to shame

Shaming yourself for your weight
And your out-of-date clothes
You feel like less of a person
And you know it shows

You don't know how to wear your smile
When you hate to see your reflection
You don't believe it is social media's fault
You see no connection

The apps make you so happy
But only when you get attention
It causes you to have a need for
Your peer's validation

Doing all you can to look cool
Putting forth so much effort
To get noticed in school

Noticed for your "fresh new shoes"
Or your cool hair dye
You just want compliments
From all the hot guys

But now everyone craves the attention of others
We can thank social media for that
For creating unrealistic beauty standards
And mental damage that can't be taken back

You'll forever compare yourself to others
Because of a stupid app
An app that markets off the weak
And makes us believe a bunch of dumb crap

*Charley Johnson*

# Family

F amily.
　　Supposed to be there for you
Through thick and thin.
But how is it they are the ones who hurt you most?

They speak their mind
Without even thinking.
They don't think about if they should.

Words hurt.
And they don't realize.
They are too focused on themselves to realize they are hurting
their own child.

Shaming and judging,
But it's just out of "love."
They don't want you getting hurt by the world,
So they hurt you first.

Breaking you down
And pushing you away,
Making you feel helpless and alone.
But it's just out of "love," right?

They tell you that you should lose weight
And that the dress isn't made for a body like yours.

And when you eventually build up the courage to start feeling
good in your skin,
They tear you apart.
But it's just out of "love."

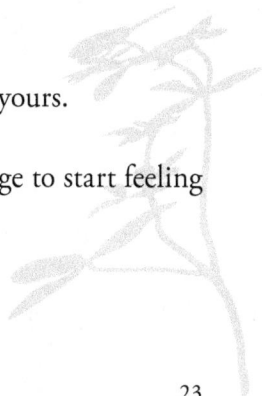

Their words echo in your head
Every second of every day.
It breaks you to pieces,
And they never go away.

They say all these words out of "love."
Well, their love hurts.

It's the love of a family member,
Not meant to be gentle and sweet,
Meant to teach you that life and love
Are not like they are in fairy tales

For they are not there to be your friend.
They are there to be your parents.

But being a parent should still consist of a feeling of safety.
But it feels like a black hole,
Swallowing you alive without rest.

No breath for air,
Suffocated by their "love."

*Charley Johnson*

# Heartbreak #1

Words.
Empty and meaningless.
Even those meant for the strongest of feelings.
Their meaning supposed to portray a deep bond,
A bond in which should not be breakable.
But even the smallest of cracks can bring everything crumbling down.

Crashing and shattering
Unable to be fixed
Broken.
That strong bond meant to withstand storms and overcome mountains has crumbled.

And with it a heart.
The heart of the vulnerable
Not strong enough to succumb to the possibility of a bad ending,
For they only believe in fairy tales.
Not reality.

Reality hurts
It is not for the weak,
Yet she was given a fake glimpse,
A glimpse of what she wants most
Love.

Without the accusation of heartbreak
For it couldn't happen to her,
Right?
Wrong.

He put forth a fake mask
Covering what he was capable of.
He could break her into a million pieces with few words,
For trust can get you anywhere.

The girl.
Now weak, broken, and more vulnerable,
Only wanting someone to be there for her.

So when the destroyer shows back up,
Over
And over again,
She believes him when he says he has changed.

Empty apologies for his harm,
She is just a place holder for him,
Someone to take up time before the next girl.

But to her, he is the whole world.
Perfection.
Could that be so far from the truth.

For she longs for one thing
His love.
She knows it's fake.
She knows what he's capable of
But will do anything for the feeling of love again.

But broken love only breaks more.
She recovered what she could from the first heartbreak
Just to be destroyed countless more times by the same boy.

He knows what he's doing.
He knows.
Love is a fantasy,
Unrealistic and harmful.
But after a glimpse of it,
You are stuck with the longing for more.

# Heartbreak #2.
# What Is Love?

D on't you hate it when you think you feel certain words
But can't bring yourself to say them,

Afraid of scaring off the other person
By saying them too early and ruining what could be?

When you have waited every past time,
But never quite got to that point before destruction,

Before everything came crashing down
Because of your self-destruction.

Yet you can't rid of the feeling,
Of the thought of what if that is what you feel.

When everything is confusing you,
And you change your mind every next minute
Because you can't help but overthink everything that crosses
your mind.

*Charley Johnson*

So, in all you can't rid of the thought of the feeling
Of thinking what if it is,
But you fear the destruction coming again
Because it happens every time.

You can't help it.
You try and try,
Yet... nothing.

No one seems to be able to prevent it,
Prevent the crashing of everything built,
The crumbling of every feeling created.

# Written in Stone

I once wrote out my feelings.
The feelings I had for you.
I wrote them on a napkin.
Not the most convenient, but in writing.

Then you got with her.
I was filled with hurt.
Rage.
I tore up that napkin.
Those feelings gone.
Yet something didn't feel right.
Those feelings were still there.

I wrote out my feelings.
The feelings I had for you.
This time on paper.
I kept it in my back pocket.
Close to me.
The way I wish you were.

I saw you and her holding hands,
sharing hugs,
the way you smiled at her.

I tore up the paper.
And with it my feelings for you.
Gone.
Yet the thought of you still there.

*Charley Johnson*

I wrote out my feelings.
The feelings I didn't know I still had for you.
Except in pen.
Written in permanent ink in the back of my notebook.

You are always a distant memory.
What we had.
What we could've had.
But it's over.

So I tore out that page.
Set the page to flames.
That permanent ink destroyed.

I thought I was over you.
I thought.

I wrote out my feelings.
The feelings I had for you.
The feelings I can't rid of.

I carved them into stone.
Chipping away at it.
Similar to how your actions chip at my heart.
You hurt me.

I couldn't get over you.
You were always there.
You were.

I threw the stone to the ocean.
Open blue skies that collided with the blue sea.
The never-ending horizon that faded into sunset.

The stone.
A relic of what I did feel for you.
Gone.

I wrote out an apology.
An apology for the way I acted.
The way things ended.
An apology for me.
I wrote it down on a napkin.
It may not be permanent,
but I mean everything I wrote.

*Charley Johnson*

# Your Love

H eat.
It's comforting.
The warmth from a fire.
The warmth from a hug.
Cozy blankets, fuzzy socks, hot sand.

Fire.
Fire is heat.
But not always comforting.
Flames rising tall, surrounded.
Smoke filling the air, suffocated.
Fire.

Your love is like fire.
Dangerous.
Harmful.
Painful.
It destroys everything in its path.
Destruction.

It once was like heat.
Safe.
Warm.
Loving.
All that changed in seconds.

That candle I lit for you broke.
And everything was set to flames.
Unbearable.
You hurt me.
Constantly.
The fire did damage.
You weakened me.

Your flames burnt my structure.
I am unstable.
The smallest push makes a crack.
Cracks add up.
They result in a crumble.

And even after all that.
Your memories are salvageable.
Your warm feel.
Our shared laughs.
Our love.

It was ours.
I was building that house for us.
Us.
What we could have had.

Now I must rebuild it on my own.
For me.
There is no more us.
We were set to flames.
Burned.
Our love to ashes.
Blown away with the wind.

*Charley Johnson*

I pick up shards of glass.
The glass from your candle.
Cutting my hands as I collect them.
You continue to hurt me.
It never ends.

Yet still I will not rid of your memory.
Those pictures, hoodies, jewelry, and glass will be saved.
Tucked away in a box.
Pushed away, while I rebuild myself.

You will always be there.
A distant thought.
A memory.

I choose to only remember your candle.
Not your flames.
Your heat.
Not your fire.

# The Light We Shine on our Mental Fights

L ife can be tough, and it has its many struggles. However, you should never give up. Although it may seem like nothing will get better, trust me, it will. God only gives people struggles he knows they can handle. For it can't rain forever. After cold dreary storms comes the warm comforting rays from the sun, and maybe even the vibrant colors from a rainbow. So just remember, you are not alone. We all face similar hardships and should not feel ashamed to ask for help. Sometimes someone to talk to can make the biggest difference in your day-to-day life. There are also many resources that are here specifically to help you. Day or night, you can always call and someone will be there to talk to you as long as you need. Use any online website to find the hotline for you. You are loved. Never forget that. ☺

*Charley Johnson*

www.ingramcontent.com/pod-product-compliance
Lightning Source LLC
LaVergne TN
LVHW051609080426
835510LV00020B/3206